Alluring Thoughts in the Mind of a Poet

I0151320

MOVE OUT PUBLISHING HOUSE

COPYRIGHT

CONTENTS

CONTENTS

CONTENTS

CONTENTS

Peach

After her peach,
No peach
Ever tasted
The same...

Say My Name

Say My Name.

Not because of dominance.
I just want to confirm
That Angels walk the earth
Covered in skin,
Like Nubians,
And Eyes Full Of Fire.

Speak,
So that I may observe in life
What I've always imagined in moments of manifestation.

Say My Name
And Complete Me;

Say My...

CREAM

I gave her the world, but didn't factor in my time.
I used my money like get out of jail free cards.
But that wasn't what she was looking for.
She wanted me;
Not what I could purchase.
I just lost my angel to the root of all evil...

That C.R.E.A.M.

Mental G-spot

You mind if I touch your G-Spot?

I know without guessing, you assumed I was speaking of that
beautiful place which lies beyond the doorway of your legs
that reveals the place that most call heaven.

I must say, today you thought wrong. Because, where I want
to touch is a little above shoulder length and requires no
physical interaction at all.
Just an open ear that is ready and willing to hear the
expressions of thought I'd like to share and watch you act out.

I'm trying to mentally penetrate you. For a moment, I'd like for
you to be an adjective and myself an adverb.
Let me qualify you by expressing the relation of my word flow
and your mental stimulation.

I'm trying to verbally massage your central nervous system,
arousing your senses to the extent of overload.
I want you to visualize being at the edge of a cliff and to reach
your peak;

All you'd need do is leap.

Not yet, though. I'm not into doing anything prematurely and we have plenty of exploring to do.
You feel me yet?
Have you already imagined my hands on you?
Where are they?
How do they feel?

It's ok to close your physical eyes to get a better picture.
I've already Opened Your Third Eye. Since you decided to sit here, I've been communicating with you telepathically. I must say, the discussion between your third eye and I is quite enticing.

I didn't anticipate our mental foreplay to be this intense I'm sure.
Your mention of moist palms and lip biting gave you away.
But that's ok. Because, in my mind, I've been sampling you like dessert cups at an ice cream shop on a hot day.

I'm indecisive about my toppings so I'll try them all on you.
The strawberry was too sweet. Plus, I like the real thing.
The caramel was good, but didn't fit the moment.

Now that chocolate... Ooohhh, that oh-so-perfect chocolate!
Seems to be melding with your skin, giving me the most delectable gift of goodness I'd ever placed in my mouth. That's where you melted.
That's where I wanted you.
Not in my hands.
Not anywhere else, but where you were supposed to be.

I was grateful. I could tell you were, too, because I kept at it even after.
I guess this explains the moist palms, soon to be followed by other areas - depending on the level of mental pleasure.

I'm just trying to show you more than most and not anything less than what you deserve.

So again I'll ask;
You mind if I touch your G-Spot?

Blue Moonlight

Under the full blue moon; she pleases herself, calling to me with her moans.
I refuse to reply at first.
I'm too busy enjoying the show in front of me.

To make it more enticing, I grab my favorite oils to rub her down with. Jasmine and lavender scents take up the room.
As the oils drip down from the small of her back to the top of the shoulders her natural juices splash to the floor.
Firm, but gentle, hands work the oils into every groove enjoying the beauty of God's work.

Vigorously, you stroke your purity anticipating your essence to flow out. My touches are embraced as you continue to moan my name pleading for me to enter you.
As your climax became nearer, it seemed as if the moon itself was becoming brighter.

Wanting to please you, I removed your hand and replaced it with my tongue to ensure your best experiences.
In my mind, I was made to please you, so all of my efforts are given.
The motion your body is swaying in informs me you're at the moment of sheer bliss.

Your breaths become heavier. My movements, even faster.
Your arch, so much deeper. Your heart, I bet its racing.
This feeling! It's so exciting, the anticipation is killing me.
Our bodies jerking so violently! Real beauty is taking place.
Passion. It's all over your face, right before you yell out!

It was nothing I'd ever heard. Like joining with your animal
spirit, howling at the moon. I'm just grateful to be apart of
your experience, under the blue moonlight.

Body Canvas

In an artsy mood, I decided to paint a picture. I started off on a
blank board but your body looked like a better canvas.
Unknown to me, at first, I was using edible paint. But, after
all, there are no mistakes. So I feel like these brush strokes of
desire were already predestined to take place.

I kissed your yoni first, to heat up your body, because I
wanted the paint to stick perfectly. Using my tongue as a
second paint brush, I gently brush back and forth past your
clit; not forgetting to suck lips on the down stroke. As I'm
doing so, I'm painting your thighs a fiery red and orange, to
signify the heat that is growing in both of our lower regions
and going up our chakras like the gauge on a thermometer.

You are hot and the combined energy is so amazing. You
place me in your hands and feel my shared heat, whispering
"Let me cool you" while taking me into your mouth and
making me feel free. With each inch that disappears in and out
of your mouth, you continue to suck as I pulsate and you feel
it so you go faster. My body cannot take it and all it wants is
you.

Paint and paint brushes are thrown to the floor and we dive in them creating a love story with only our bodies.

I straddle, fiercely pumping into you all of me and you take it with so much desire for me, the sensation is so unbelievable. We switch as you decide to ride it out. Swirling and grinding and swirling and grinding, then ecstasy! Your juices come down on me mixing with paint, making colors I've never seen.

As you lay on my chest we look around to enjoy the picture we painted together. There is a pause of peace and beauty. Just to think; it started with a paint brush.

Faults

Looked for faults in you, because
I was honestly insecure with
myself.

I figured, if I pushed you far enough away, I'd be right about me.
You wouldn't leave though. You just kept loving me.

Where I seen failure, you somehow seen the real ME. The Me I had
forgotten about. The Me I made
think love wasn't real.

She waits for me.
She lusts for me in the darkest parts of her mind.
I am her secret.
When she is alone, she drips for me.
Only for me.

I rub down her saturated gateway with one finger.
Eye contact.
I taste her.
She moans for me.
She is sweet.
I like that.
I have her taste her too.
She bites her lip.
Moans escape lips while hand travels down temple to reach
places of no return.

She's alive now.
Body moving to music that is not present, but keeping the
rhythm to the groove in the soul.
She calls for me.
Not one word was spoken.
Her aura did the talking.
I am awake now.
She has released her pheromones.
Her seductive actions elicit a reaction from my manhood.

I am hers now.
She was never really mine.
Persuaded into assumptions of dominance.
I sit here before her. A slave to her ecstasy.

I am hers now... She likes that...

The Alpha

As the sheets rubbed passed her naked skin, she fantasized of a love to grip her curves like a glove would a hand.

Kisses were imagined against her skin from a king that has earned her soul. Thighs touch, anticipating the warmth of a lover that will please her the right way.

This lioness wants to be preyed on by the lion. Not just any lion. The Alpha.

You Owe Me

You owe me.

Give me back all the love I put
into you. Including every single
call where I stayed on the phone
with you, just to hear you sleep, so
you wouldn't feel alone.

I want back every note, every kiss, every stroke I placed
across your skin.

I want the other part of my soul back that I dedicated to you.

Why, you ask?

Because you broke me and I
Need to relearn how to love me again...

If Death Comes For Me

If death comes for me,
Let it be Her kiss that sends me
Into the unknown,
Her words that guide me,
And Her love that gives comfort.
Until we meet again.

Play In Her Hair

Nothing like when you're taking your braids down and you ask me to assist you. I shy away, but your eyes let me know the choice was never mine.

Being gentle as possible, I place comb in hand and pick out my first braid. Working my way to your scalp, I can't help but to rub my hand through the already taken out area. While you're thinking it's to sooth the pain of your scalp, have my own guilty pleasures to appease.

I love running my hands through your hair, listening to you moan from the relaxing mini-massage my fingertips give you. Subtly hearing you say "That's my spot", like we're making love and not taking hair down.

Continued conversations while we work, braid by braid, bringing us closer together. An unintentional bonding moment. The experience has taken me beyond the hair and landed me at the door of the real You. The natural, strong Queen I grew to cherish and appreciate.

You showed me strength didn't just come from the physical, but from the heart. You are more than just your hair and I love you for that. I couldn't be pleased enough with this experience of helping you take your hair down.

Mental Gratification

I want to lick your mind, like
most say they'd lick your clit,
& give you the same sensation.

I just want you to enjoy the
pleasure of some mental gratification,
Instead of the first thing being focused
on is your physical stimulation.

I Don't Want Your Sex

I laid her down, but it wasn't
because I wanted her sex.
I wanted to rest my head
on her chest and remember,
with each beat, how I knew
God was real.

Forgive Me

You've gotten cold on me and all I think about is ways to get you warm. Your silence bites at my skin,
Like cold wind in the middle of winter.
I want to love you, but your posture is defensive.

I do what I can to sway a mood I created with my own insecurities.
Not thinking, I let out words I didn't mean, to make you feel low as I did.

Honestly, I'd rather be covered in your lips. Those kisses consume as you lay on me with your thigh on mine, making me feel whole. Not having that right now burns my soul.

What I wouldn't give to play in your hair and write poetry on how each strand made me feel. What lengths I wouldn't go through to show you I love you then make love to you and make each stroke a personal apology.

Oh, how I'd kiss and bow at your feet to show submission and complete reform from my ignorance. Just say something!

I know you care; because I see in your movements, you feel me.
So please, feel my sincerity.

I want my happy ending back;
I can't have that without you.

Answer The Phone

Answer the phone, baby.
I promise to slow the stroke so you can answer properly.
I'll be sure to be gentle to it, as you say hello, then it slide it back in slow.

I wonder if the caller hears your breathing changing, as you try to hold back the sensation of my dick sliding across your clit.
You try to cover moans by humming songs but the songs don't make sense because you're holding the note too long. You slap my thigh signaling me to slow down but, like a horse, I speed up.

Now you're pressing the phone against your chest; trying to muffle the sounds of flesh connecting as I feel your pussy contracting, conforming to my manhood as you cum, and cum hard! All while holding the phone.

I hope you've learned your lesson, about answering the phone...

Fear of Bridges

She was the woman that turned my thoughts into motivation.
Her presence gave me Nostalgia, like old jazz.
She was peace and I wanted her for so long I could feel my
past lives telling me she was the one.

Why couldn't I tell her? But I could write a manifesto of my
love for her to the world; as long as she didn't read it.

 The fear of bridges kept me in place because it was secure. To
walk this bridge, to meet her, would be well worth it. But what
if I'm not enough for her? My thoughts bind me with a rope of
doubt and make my thinking less than judicious.

I'm hard on myself when it comes to her; this is why her
bridge scares me. I could imagine each step being life
changing, each exhale harder than the one before, so breath is
held to reserve courage. I will not let this moment pass me. I
cannot let fear move me.

I will walk this bridge. Not for me, but for us because I hold
her future in my hands too. If I don't walk this bridge; I will
have failed for the both of us...

I take the step.

Self Image

It's too bad when you've changed
everything about yourself I adored
and claimed it as an imperfection.

I never seen someone so beautiful
assume they were so ugly. I wish
I could kiss your doubt away. I
would literally take my time and
kiss every lie that you told yourself
away.

It wouldn't even be a memory;
I would forever hold those burdens
for you.

Heart Missing

How do you expect me to make love
to you and your heart missing?

You must want me to fall into your
empty space and become a part of that
graveyard you've been digging...

Sweets

Yoni trapped in chocolate,
I'm stuck with a sweet tooth that only craves you.

I'd bite my way through,
But I'm more interested in
How many licks it would take
Before I reached my prize
And how many more before
Your juices squirted me.

I know I'm nasty, but so what!
Feed me my dessert first;
I'm skipping dinner tonight.

I want what I want
And you can't stop me.

Honestly, I know you don't want to.

Third Eye Love

I received you as you embraced my kisses and unwind my
mind, while intertwining legs give way to love that exist on
higher planes.

Our third eyes make love while we watch. I see your juices
flow, so I embrace you. Not to penetrate you, I just want to
watch your melanin sweat in anticipation.

You beg for me to do all of the things that my mind is doing to
your mind and repeat them on your body.

I ran my fingers through your hair then grabbed, pulled your
head back and leaned forward - whispering in your left ear...
"In due time."

She came and puddles hit the floor

Run To Me

It wasn't that I did anything wrong,
that put doubt in her;
it was me doing everything right.

So many let downs lead her to
believe I'd be just another one. She tried to leave, to spare
herself
the pain, but I refused to let go.

I explained that I knew her hurt
and I would not unleash it; instead
let love live if she'd only believe
it.

I'm trying to change last names,
not bedside stories, so stop running
away from me; run to me.

Seeing Sex In Color

As my girth grew inside her, she took my fingers into her
mouth; to silence her moans and to pacify her seduction.
Hips moved like ocean waves, stroking spots she had long
assumed nonexistent.

Ass claps on thighs sound like thunderstorms approaching
causing those in fear to take cover.
But you, you choose to ride the storm out.

You had no idea it was a category five and that it would leave
that pussy in a state of emergency. You've been flooded out; I
opened up your metaphoric dam and let the flood waters loose.

From then on, you promised to never take me lightly. You
found a new respect for me and now you can't get enough me.

I've become your satisfaction and that, in itself, is enough for
me. I'm glad you've enjoyed your ride.

Angry Poem

**I wrote this note when I was angry & in anguish so you
knew, for sure, that my words would be true.
My love for you is undying. I know I'm raising my voice, but
please pay more attention to the context. **

I love you; you have given a part of me life that I thought long
deceased.

You have awaken happiness that I never want to go back to
sleep.

You have done things; I mean really done things that have changed the entire spectrum of my being.
You changed my perspective on trust. It was always "keep one eye open"

But for you, for you I close both and let you lead the way. As I said; I know I'm raising my voice but please, please pay more attention to the context.

I love you. You have given a part me life that I thought long deceased.

As the tears flow from my eyes, believe me it's not for sympathy, but you made it ok to feel again.
I was taught to not show weakness; you showed me that showing my emotions was not where the weakness lies; it was the lack of that showed real truth.

You have set me free...
Thank You.

When Role Play Goes Right

You've been bad. What should your pleasure, I mean your punishment be?

How bad have you really been?
Are you going to tell me, or do I have to work it out of you?
Smack!

As I slap her on the ass, her ass cheek she goes to grab while she moans and then she laughs then says
"Oh Daddy, I mean officer, is that all you have?"

My reply was

"Oh, I see we have a wise ass. Let's see what happens when the night stick comes out and I crown you?"

I pull it out and then she gasps...

When role playing goes right.

A Night To Remember

As the rain hits the windows, I try intensely to keep up with the beat it creates as Mother Nature pours down its rainfalls. The clapping of thunder slightly covers the whimpers of passion expressed as you take everything I'm giving you. The position of power I'm in allows me full accessibility to ensure you feel my true strength with every thrust that I'm giving you.

As your hands are placed on the floor and thighs continue to hang from the bed, I take my place behind you like guiding a ship from the helm. As I penetrate deeper, your toes twist into the sheets and your hands attempt to grip whatever little carpet it can to control the climax experienced.

Unknown to you, was the second one that came swiftly after the first. Just to think, all this before I've tasted you. Your shivers only excited me.
The gyration of those hips only made your lips wetter, my stroke better, your legs weaker, my passion greater, your voice fainter.

The once loud roars of the mighty lioness have been turned into docile purrs of satisfaction. The calm finally ensued and the storm outside has subsided. Peace has been made in the sheets.

19

Love still stains the air with a constant reminder of the events of the night.
A night to remember.

Caught In The Moment

I want to be caught in a moment so intense that our blinds are open with the nosey neighbor peeking through. I want it to be day time; no, night time with the lights on or candles lit so I can watch your silhouette as well as you receive pleasure from me.

I want your moans to be the melody, your sweat on the ground the treble and the headboard the bass. We will create the sweetest song just from our love. But it won't stop there.
We have an entire house to make our love songs. So let's not cut short what flows so well. Let's hit an intermission.

I'm going to hold your leg and thigh like a saxophone, place my mouth on your sweetness and play like my last concert before retirement.
I'm going to make the walls tremble as I play my heart out, while your humming of ecstasy takes the crowd home.
They feel you; because they're in that moment of love right with you.

My jazz is impeccable. God's gift to me to bless my Queen.
Please her; I shall, as we play our song of love.

Mentally

I heard great minds fuck each other. But for you, I'd rather take my time.

Yes, those quick, powerful swipes across the brain might be fundamental, but I'm trying to change your whole life.
I'd rather long stroke you.
Place each word in you, slowly, like inches of my penis going into that place of no return.

I'm going to embed myself in you, then spread my seed, ingraining thought that will become essential to your daily thinking. You won't even be able to go to the bathroom without thinking of me.

Wet panties will be your new name. When my name comes up, you'll beg not to hear it a third time, like Candy Man. Your candy rain won't be able to help itself. Your feelings for me will stick out, like the proverbial sore thumb.

Trying to hide the effects of the mental lovemaking I put on you would be the equivalent of trying to have a quiet orgasm; not going to happen. I'm going to be like music playing... Rest in my book coming soon

Drip For Me

I could not help but to feel her soon as I hit the room. Body glistened like wet paint. Now that I think of it, more like wet cherries that had just been sprayed at the grocery store.

Either way, I knew I wanted to lick her. From her back dimples to her collarbone, from her collarbone to her delicious center, from that center I would enter her and when I entered her, I'd make sure she would remember.

I'd dig deep. I'd inch inside her until I heard the sound of her losing air. Not an exhale; that sound you hear when pain and pleasure meet and you can't decide which one you want more.

She wanted me to punish her. She wanted swift strokes, bite marks and bad names. I wanted to lift her up, beat it up, fold her up, eat it up, put it back in, and then eat again.

I needed her so satisfied from me she would be numb to the touch of another man. It would be pointless to ever come behind me and think you ever had a chance to please her like I can.

She will only drip for me

Superwoman

She said I couldn't see her tears in the rain, but she didn't realize I could feel them as if they were falling from my own face. Smiles hide so many scars that most forget she's human too. Even Super Woman needed saving.

Don't disregard her femininity because she lacks the ability to show sensitivity. It doesn't mean she lacks the ability; maybe she is not given the luxury.

Tattoos cover heartbreaks, mistakes and every moment of rage she felt she couldn't take, along with every success time blessed and memories of happiness she'd never change. Her Godliness is embedded in every line stroke so there is no mistaking the beauty that is her name.

22

How I wish I could hold her soul and tell her I see her so she wouldn't feel so alone. To see her vessel glow gives me hope that someday; someway I'll see her smile again.

Heart Pure

Can you see that my soul is pure,
Or do you judge me on my outer appearance?

Will I ever be free?
Will I ever be accepted?
As the king my ancestors told me I am?
Or will I be locked in the shackles
Of my colored skin?

You see it as a curse,
I see it as a badge of honor.
I wear my blackness with pride.

Soul Connections of Love

What love making is to me, when it comes to soul connections.

You don't just enter her; you breathe her, you take her in and watch your energy exhaled. You spiritually start to take one form and feel as if you're leaving this dimension to be one in another.

Each kiss is like witnessing what, in my mind, would be the feeling of being a supernova. The energy is so powerful that you doubt the existence of the moment being real until you touch each other again. You start to see colors. You feel the flowing juices transferring from one another. Even sweat is sweet.

23

This type of intimacy is not easily captured, but forever remembered. I apologize for the rambling; got caught in a moment.

The Conversation

I subconsciously tapped a Queen on her third eye with my own. I wanted her to know I seen her light and wanted to multiply it then divide it amongst our people.

I said to her "I want to be your Asar (Osiris), only if you promise to be my Aset (Isis). I can't accept anything less than a Queen."

She told me "Not only will I be your Aset, but if you depart from this world I'll resurrect you through your words. It will be my mouth, but your spirit will move me. You will never die."

She took my hand and asked me if I was good with that? I replied "That's peace, come walk with me."

True Beauty

True beauty is when you Wake Up
And realize God gave you
All the makeup you needed.
She named it skin.

Inhaled

I inhaled her essence
and finally knew peace.

My Soul

Kiss my soul
Not my ego

Soul Selfie

I asked if she could take a selfie
of her soul, so I'd know who I was
dealing with. Because that Mac
makeup has been known to be
good for concealing shit.

She told me she wasn't ready for
that type of commitment. Then she
threw her ass in the air and told me
"But you can have this".

I kindly declined, there was no way I
was attaching my soul to her battered womb for a lifetime...
LIFETIME

Good Hair

Frustrated, she refused to turn to me. All that was in sight was hoop earrings and beautiful wavy hair the color of moor. Waves deep as those that crashed onto African shores, bringing great oppression like the comments the Queen faced daily.

"This isn't your real hair, this has to be weave. If not weave, then texturized".

Her response is always the same;
"Yes, this is mine and sorry it's not texturized. I just take good care of my hair. By the way, I'm not mixed - just in case you were about to fix those lips to insult me any further. I'm a full Black Queen and I love me for me and you should try doing the same".

The ignorance from those that were cultureless upset her. She just wanted to be free in her own black skin without assumption of her how she is not being enough to be the beauty you see before you.

I seen that she had it rough, so I did not give her a hard time or ask once more for her to turn around.

I simply told her
"You are beautiful just the way you are."
Then walked away. I didn't look, but I could feel her smile. I was content.

Ugly

I've never physically
seen an ugly person,
not until they opened
their mouth.

Feed Off Her Knowledge

I had lost my appetite altogether
until I tasted her knowledge and
became hungry.

I placed face under
her lips in hopes of catching jewels
that escaped those that were hard
of hearing.

I could mentally stimulate
myself to her synonyms and make
love to her metaphors; she is the
complete package with her clothes on.

I just wanted her to speak to me in tongues and pour her
knowledge all over.
She is my full plate of knowledge.
I am ready to feast!

Light in a Dark Room

You are the light in a dark room
And a part of my soul loves you for it.

Unseen Beauty

I followed this woman through a
crowd of people because, to me, she
stood out above them. Some would
have called her mediocre. But they
didn't see her through clear eyes.

I reached her and let her know, "If no one in this room sees
you; I do.
I want you to know you're beautiful".

Her smile did what the sun wished
 it could only do if but once...
Light up the world.

It Just Is

The thing about love is;
it was never physical,
it never had a price,
Or an expiration date.

It just is.

Don't ever throw the
Most powerful thing in the world
in a box and then label it.

My love is pure, wild and unknown.
But, you can feel it,
You can feel it...

I Met God, She's Black

I met God, she's black.
It was beautiful to see her and she looks like me.

I met God, she's black.
Her blackness filled a void in me that made my soul whole.

I met God, she's black.
Not just black, but beautiful - and it made me feel beautiful
too! My skin finally meant something more than evil; it was
the beginning of the light.

I met God, she's black.
Powerful was her presence and she made me feel powerful
too!
Something about her gave me hope.
The love that came raining off her skin gave me chills that
started from within & worked its way out to my own black
skin.

I met God, she's black.
Powerful is she, but never abuses her strength.

I met God, she's black.
She told me "Never be ashamed of who you are again. Love
yourself, like you love me. We are one in the same."

I met God, she's black.

Collide

Come here and let me hold you
So tight, that we forget
What the feeling of loneliness felt like.

Let me share your air.
Touch lips to mine
And watch stars align
And melanin collide;
Creating a new world
From our love alone.

Look Within

When you awoke, did you remind
your vessel to thank its soul
for its existence?

Did you embrace yourself like you'd want another to when
you felt you needed it?

Did you believe in yourself before
asking another to?

When you see your image, do you see your greatness?
Or do I have to remind you?

I know that you are beautiful.
But I need you to know - without me
reminding you.

Compilation Album

She is the perfect addition to my
compilation album of life.

She gives me the neo-soul I was
looking for.

That record that hits you with the smooth base drop and the
soulful hymns.

She is the music that makes the world listen.

A perfect addition to my
compilation album.

I Saw Your Chakras

I saw your chakras catch fire for
me with just eye contact.

I imagined our energies intertwining like ancient dragons
doing the dance of love. Right now, I'm lusting. I can't stop
what is or what soon will be.

All I know is, I want to embrace you with all of me. Your
body is saying the same, so why deny the pleasures that have
risen from within?

Let me take you and spoil your body; give you kisses from
your root chakra all the way to your crown. Allow me to alter
your existence on earth.

Just tell me where I can start.

Teach Me

"Take me, make my body your playground and my pussy
your favorite toy,"

I replied, "I will do nothing of
that manner because that is
not my motive. I do not see you
as a toy, but a sanctuary. You're
beautiful & your pussy, as you
liked to describe it, would not
be my favorite toy - but a paradise,
a heaven in a sense, that I would
not enter until you knew my
mind loved you."

She froze & cried tears from every ocean.

She asked me "Why didn't my father
teach me these things?"

I don't know, but I'M HERE NOW.

Told You My Soul

I've told you my soul. I've come clean with you but you still
refuse to love me.

She replied
"The sun dies every night, so that the moon can arise. The
moon knows what the sun has done for her, but is still forever
alone because she knows no one will love her as much as the
sun does.

"If I admit to loving you, it would permit pain to come in, if I lost you. I am not strong as the moon. I could not take losing you once, let alone thousands of times! So, I choose to be forever alone."

I replied
"With your words, you've just killed me a thousand times."

Sun Made Love to The Moon

One evening, I watched the sun make love to the moon and became aroused. I wanted to turn away but couldn't. The way the moon wrapped herself around the sun and became one was so amazing and sensual.

All the power the sun contained and yet, still so submissive to the moon's darkness that it created around it. As I watched on, the sun slowly slipped his masculine energy into her feminine. At the peak of this moment, I finally found out how eclipses were made.

It was the orgasm of the moon.
The combined essence of the two; as the sun gave the moon all he had and seemed to want nothing in return, but to be engulfed in her blackness.

Right then, I knew I'd been lied to about the black darkness being bad. I knew right then that, if the sun would give all his power to the beauty of the darkness the moon brought, how could it be bad? How could the beautiful darkness not be the true light?

Being grateful for what I had witnessed, I had only one thought after; finding my own moon. My own darkness that would wrap me in her love for lifetimes.

Creator of Creation

They say your woman should be
your backbone. I say she should be my equal.

I may be the head, but she is the
legs that move me.
I may have the final say, but she
was the thought behind the action.
My woman is more than a backbone.

She is the creator of creation.

Keep going

Sometimes a push isn't always a push. It's a cry for help, in a
different form.

I keep going...
Even after you deny me entry.

I keep going...
After you push me away.

I keep going...
Ignoring your hurtful words that cause
internal tears.

I keep going...
Because, when I was in the exact same
space,
You kept going for me too!

Never thought calling a woman "Queen" would be fighting words, until I stepped into the 21st century.
Never imagined "Bitch" would be a compliment once I placed the word "Bad" in front of it.

I must truly be behind the times when, now, Bad means Good and Bitch is even better.

When did my fellow brother become so insecure in himself, that another man addressing his woman by her proper title became disrespectful?

Please direct me to the point, in time, where Queen became a word of flirtatious advancement.
Show me the boy that felt respect was disrespect, being passive on his true history was not neglect and to belittle a wombman was a form of praise.
Please point me to this time in history, so I may slap the shit out of him so our future can be a better place.

Now sadly, when I look in these young Queens' eyes, they are truly flattered by having the opportunity to be man's best friend. Yes, a Bitch. The bottom one, at that. Or the main Hoe.

Last, but not least, a Thot.
How did the name of a prolific part of our history become a way to disrespect our Queens? How did the creator of writing and many other wondrous things be turned into something negative? How did Thoth even fit in the category of putting down our women?

Where did things go wrong, so we can make it right? How can I fix this injustice? What must be done to bring my Queens back to greatness?

Whatever the cost, I am willing to bare it. That's just how dedicated I am to my people, to my Queens!

Her High

She let me enter in her life
like drugs would a vein.

I was her high; she couldn't get
enough of me. The satisfaction
of our relationship was beautiful.
Then the high came down and it
was a bad trip to the bottom.

I suddenly stopped being needed.
She became more distant. Then I
found why - she had stepped out
on me with rehab.

The worst day, yeah it was the worst day. I just wanted to be needed.

I See You, Black Woman

I see you black woman.
I see you and I adore you. From the ivory whites of your feet,
to your melanin crown.

I see you and I love you black woman; in all shades, all sizes,
all styles. I love you from your tight curls to your dreadlocks,
your head wraps and bantu knots.

There is not one part of you that I'd not worship. In my eyes, you are the reason the sun rises and sets. The earth revolves around your will.

I can't display or express how much you mean to me black woman, but I'll live my life trying to show you through my actions. You need not change a thing; you truly make my heart sing, Black Woman.

Black woman you complete me. Because in you, creation started - you sacrificed youth to ensure youth survived. I see your tired hands, your scarred back, your hurt feet... but you still keep going so I will too.

Black woman, as I said before, I love you. Thank you for loving me and teaching me how to love myself.

Black Woman.

Peculiar

My friends found me weird because
I'd rather slip into a woman's
thoughts than her skirt.

While they satisfied themselves off
 physical stimulation, I was searching for her essence so I
could give her true stimulation.

I wanted to move her far beyond physically; it was much too easy.
The goal for me was to be so
intertwined with her, mentally;
her soul would jerk her towards

me before her eyes had time to
see me.

What good is love if you have not captured her essence?
What good is a poem if you haven't
put your heart in it?

Too deep

"You went too deep, you went way
too deep this time. I should have
not permitted you to dive into
me so deeply that I feel you in
my footsteps.

No individual should be allowed to
be where you are in my thoughts.
How dare you find the secret place,
where I hold my fears, doubts &
insecurities, but not be kicked out?!

My mind welcomed you, even against
my judgment. Why are you here?
What is your purpose? Please don't add yourself to my heart
breaks."

I just want to free you.

In one breath, she felt peace.

Butterscotch

She is my butterscotch.
I know the consequence of her delectable sweetness, but I
indulge anyway.

When the pain comes from my
sweet desires, I've already made up
 my mind it was worth it.

That delicious butterscotch satisfies me.
She puts my sweet cravings at ease.

She Is

A woman is more
Than the pleasures
That lie inside her.

She is more
Than just
An inanimate object
To be used
At leisure.

She is more
Than a bad bitch.

She is heaven.
She is birth.
She is us.
She is we.
She is you.

I Love You Because

There aren't too many words,
Outside of amazing,
That would help describe you.

But my plan is to diligently search
For some that come close.

When I do find these words,
I will write poetry for you.
All of them will start with
"I Love You Because..."

Figure 8

Imagine me loving you
For the rest of your life.

Then multiply that
By how many lives I'd reincarnate
Just to fall in love with you
One more time.

You are my infinity.
8

You

I admire you
For finding beauty
Even in the eyes of darkness.

I, myself,
Find the beauty I need
In you.

Verge

My eyes are warm because you gave me life. Your soft touch
brought back senses that I assumed were not needed, because
of constant misuse.

Your touch is surreal, but, it was your eyes that really did it for
me. They would tell me they loved me and those lips would
seal the deal.

You told me I was your addiction; it's passed that for me.
You've become life.

Each breath I take is a silent I love you. I'm ready to start a life
with you too.

Empyrean

I filled a bowl with your juices because I wanted a little piece of heaven to myself. I drank from you and was able to see the universe in your reflection.

You took my soul to another dimension, where secret knowledge was hidden and stars came to die by giving their light to the world turning supernova.

You made love to me here right on top of constellations resembling ancient mathematics while pressing on my third eye. You gave me life, with each stroke my chakras lit up finally matching yours. Our auras so bright, the stars seemed to become jealous as our true connection has finally been made.

Finally I see her, even though my eyes are closed and that's when she returned me to myself. She explained that we were one now and that our connection could never be severed.

I not only tasted heaven, she became one with me and I with her. Our love would live on forever.

I'm Lonely Without You

My lotus, I grow weak in your absence. Beauty has no real meaning when you have left from eyesight. Food has lost its feeling of nourishment. The sun set that we used to enjoy, has brought, me only sadness. The sunrise we made love under made me feel even more alone.

I grip tightly to the blanket you used to wrap up in to sit and listen to my poetry. I inhale, trying to take in any feeling of you being close to me. I am finding it harder and harder to appreciate life when you are what gives me life.

That is the true reason behind why I call you my lotus. I hope in time I receive a reply, because these days you are away are literally killing me.

Anata ga inaito sabishii desu... (I'm lonely without You...)

Lost key

Smeared makeup, waterfalls start as streams but, this time, they were created from heartbreak.

Soul in disarray, he told me he lost my key and did not want to find it again, lied to me again, said he would protect the key to my heart with his life; guess he died again.

Facts conflict with denial, creating confusion because I'm in disbelief of my reality. This has to be an alternate dimension where all sad things happen to me and soul mates break promises. Like the pilgrims who broke break with Amerindians in the name of peace; but no peace ensued, just pieces of me scattered and diseased with the sickness of sadness.

I am torn... I am torn and my eyes won't stop creating waterfalls. I'm drowning in sorrow and you're standing there with a face and look dry as desserts. Like our love meant nothing. I thought my kisses were irreplaceable. I thought my hugs gave you hope.

Who's going to play in my hair? Who's going to kiss me before bed, like you do? Never thought I had to imagine counting the stars with anyone else but you.

Now all I have are moments I can grab temporary happiness from, that now end in pain. The thought of you hurts, but oddly keeps me sane.

"What makes you laugh can make you cry" has never been more real, than in this moment.

I'm hurting; my mind is in a thick fog so I do what I do best, I skate. I skate to escape it all. I skate to feel free and unbroken. I am free. Picture from model and complete bad ass.

My Day

I know this is my day to rejoice
for love & companionship,
but I want every person to
know love like this.

To know they have a piece
of life's beautiful desire.
Someone to love you back.

What's Your Name

Just wanted to connect with your
Mental and conversate with your soul, but you continue to attempt to
tempt me with flesh.

You must understand, that it's not
where my love lies. My arousal was
to your mental, so please put
your clothes back on and reward me
with conversation.

44

Don't take it as you not being beautiful. I just found more
beautiful things about you that I'd like to explore first.

I'm an old soul, so let me earn
you like old souls used to. Let me
show you real love and good
conversation still exist.

So tell me, what's your name?

Perspective

As she judges herself in that mini courtroom, called the
bathroom, I sit in amazement of her beauty.

She says a small prayer to this inanimate object, to wish away
her tummy and hips I so love to grab before she steps on the
scale, or witness stand, to plead negatively.

Where I see wonder, she sees regret. Where I see love in her
handles, she sees excess fat. I wish she'd step away from that
visual prison cell, called a mirror, and look at her image
through my eyes and mirror it.

Baby you look great!
"You're just saying that."
Baby you killing that dress! "Yeah, but look at my back."
I love you in those jeans!
"I don't, look at my fat roll!".

I attempt to stay positive, showing no signs of how her words
affect my feelings because my rare jewel is feeling real
common when she is nothing of the sort. I'm discouraged, yet
I still slap my game face on.

45

After her third wardrobe change, I stop her. I embrace her from behind with all I have to give and say;

"You may not be the size you'd like to be, but you're getting there and I believe in you. Your body may not be as slim as you like, but when did that equal you not being beautiful?

I see beauty in what you see as flaws. I see eye candy not an eyesore. You may not be the weight you want to be, but I love you anyway. There could not be an amount you gained that would ever keep me away! I will stay.

By the way, when you've been writing your weight down, I've been changing it, you actually lost ten pounds. You didn't gain it. I know, it seems cruel, but that scale does not make the rules.

You're beautiful regardless. I just wanted you to see that too. I'm here for you."

If I

If I would have fucked you
 I would have been your favorite.

But since I made love to you,
 I'm moving too fast.

Now, when I leave you,
Don't you dare say;
"There's no good men left."

You just let one leave you.

Sunflower

She's my sunflower.
Sweet and bitter
All at once.

An acquired taste
That I can appreciate.

Cherished

I cherished her.
Not for her physical, it was how her spirit spoke to me.
Resonated deeper than any touch ever felt, any song ever
heard.

I would tell her "I love your soul"
Instead of "I love you", because to
Just love her vessel would not
Be enough. It would disrespect
Her soul and give the body the
Praise the soul earned.

I loved her from within. If
You have never felt this way,
It might be safe to say, you've
Never really loved at all.

Love At First Sight

Everything was thrown at her,
but the truth. She was so used to lies, that she abandoned the concept of
honesty. I was dedicated to changing her mind.

If she could not believe
my lips, then surely my energy
would tell the truth. As she turned away guy after guy,
not even acknowledging their
existence just a brief "no thank you",
I finally took my chances despite
my odds.

I said "Hello, what can I do
not to be like them?"
She replied "You've done it already; I felt your energy when you walked over here."

She lifted her glasses to reveal she was blind, but that did not stop her third eye from connecting with mine.

Love at first sight.

A Queen Speaks

As she stands silent, her beauty is admired and worshiped. Her energy generated surrounds and captures you like a giant aura. Power is felt in each step she takes because the Ancients walk with her.

The strength of Sekhmet and the gracefulness of Nefertiti is seen in her actions. Pure is the empress' soul because she follows the principles, or commandments, of Ma'at, all forty two; ten wasn't enough to guide her people in the direction of purity.

Her leadership is impeccable. Her spirit is unshakable. Only fear she has is the loss of her people. Not by death, but in the mind. Her soul duty, wake up the sleep. No more sheep. Time to wake. Time to take, what they took. Our ancient knowledge, our fathers, our books. Emasculated our men to stop our growth, kill our future. Dumb us down to the ground, then jail the rest of our future.

"Emancipation Proclamation is in order", the Queen says. "It's time to save our daughters. The young beauties are so delicate, so full of light. They're kind hearted, good spirited, but no fight. They lack direction. No structure, no leaders. Time to change. Make way, create leaders.

Instead of trying to fit into the category of beauty depicted, how bout you try to fit into God's depiction. You're beautiful, including internally. Fashion couldn't make you any better.

You're better than better! Skin smoother than cocoa butter that has been left in sun too long. You drip beauty. You are a flower sought after by many. This is why you have to be prepared. I am with you".

Hopefully the greatness of her presence was felt in you. The strength of her words reminded you of who you are. I pray the point of the words were not missed. I hope you realized who the Queen was in this. Yes it's you.

Just remember;
Bitch bad, Woman good, QUEEN better, make it understood.

Soul Sistah

How can I be taken seriously
about respecting a woman's spirit
if I can't even respect the vessel
 that holds it?

If I am to be followed, I shall make sure my actions are pure.
After all, how can I not love the very thing that birthed
creation?

Soul sistah, I love you.

Love Pure

To her, love was pure as sun rays
 that crept through windows
 to enjoy her skin.

She smiles at thoughts of being loved and having that happily
ever after.

I want to give it to her.
She deserves it.

Leave a Message

I knew I loved her when I tried
to call her and there was no
answer. So I professed my love to the answering machine.

When I called once more because
we had just talked and still got the same answering machine.

It was not anger I felt, but worry.
Worry that the last time we spoke would be the last time.
My heart sank, then my phone rang.
I love you.

Regret

I wanted to just exist and be left
alone.
When I got what I wanted,
it wasn't what I wanted at all.

Now I sit wishing I had someone to
sit with. Someone to call my own.

Deceived

I just wanted to wake up her spirit and show her the light. She
spent so many years in the shadows; she could not bring
herself to trust my
actions.

She'd rather take her chances holding the Devil's hand than
grab on to mine and be deceived yet another time...

Nothingness

There's some real peace that comes with the rain, that you feel with no other element.

I sometimes wonder if it is because when we are in the womb of our mothers we felt the most comforted.

I can't be sure but, whatever it is, I love to be there in that moment. I sense of peace.

Nothingness

Pour Into You

You said love was a foreign language, so I learned one for you.

"Dejame derramarme en ti,
Abrete a mi,
Para que yo puedo reemplazar
Todo lo que te han quitado. "

This is what I meant, in my heart amor,

"Let me pour into you.
Open up to me,
So that I can replace
All that has been taken away."

Let me pour back the trust
That was betrayed.
That time spent.
Those nights of love making,
That was only real on your end.

Open up to me so that
I may pour back into you
The feeling of love.

Let me replace all those
Fallen tears, let downs and
Inadequate conversations.

I want to replenish your soul.
Let me show you.

There is still hope where you see disappointment.
Still faith where you see failure.
Still power in these 3 words;
I Love You.

Lost

I went down on her with ill intent.
It was not for the pleasure,
I wanted her mind.

To add such a treasure to my
so many already, would be a win.

I am no good but she swears I'm good for her.

Lost.

Simple man

I'm a simple man;
I just want to build forts, read comic books with flashlights
and make love under skylights. Enjoy talks about the universe
while naming distant sun's after you.

She replied,
"You grab the flashlights and I'll start the fort!"

Right then, in my mind, no other
woman ever existed before or would
after. She became my alpha and omega.

The beginning of love,
The ending of doubt.

Double Standard

Has the black man become so untrusted, that a compliment
can't be given without an
assumption of flirtatious
advancement?

But disrespect is tolerated from the male and female alike.
Isn't that right "bad bitch"?
You feel me my
nigga?

Or should I just kill two
birds with one stone?
Bitch Nigga

Heartless

Had no idea you'd leave me
stranded, after I told you I
had nothing left to give.

You played with the contents

54

of my heart, like a child at
recess. Why take from me
with no intention of giving?

You are the reason for sorrow.
You are the creator of what I
now have to call my reflection.

Heartless... I hope you're happy.

Loyalty

I would break through any barrier imagined, just to stay
relevant in your heart.

I'd stand up in front of crowds of thousands just to profess my
love for you.

I'd protect you with everything I have to ensure I can awake to
you
another day.

I'm dedicated, all I ask is you stay loyal or leave me alone.

I Deserve That

I tried to run back for her.

"Too late", was what she said.

My soul ached as my head replayed the last words I heard
from my angels lips.

She only left me with memories.

I deserve that.

That Type Of Battle

Her insecurities
Were the only thing
I couldn't
Separate her from.

She seemed to even love them
More than me.

How could I win
That type of battle
On my own?

When She's Sleep

Sometimes,
When she's sleep,
I hold her hand
And whisper to her
"I love you"

It's no better feeling than to feel.

That Look

I did something once. It was truly for all the wrong reasons.
I took for that a valuable lesson.

When I did something again, I found you. This time, all my

reasons were the right ones & it showed by the way you looked at me.

That look, that Love could only identify.

Hopeless

I wanted you so much; I could
feel it in every part of my being. I could imagine us, vividly
becoming as one.

The chill of ecstasy you give
is blinding. So much so, that I had not taken the time to get to
know your soul.

That was where I went wrong.
That is where I paid the price.
I was pleasing my vessel, with every stroke I gave you. Whilst
my soul suffered because, deep down, it knew you weren't The
One.

I ignored my intuition. Now I'm soul searching again.
Hopeless.

Earth

There used to be something about
about a woman that made you
want to praise them, appreciate them, adorn them. I'll be glad
when that comes back, so I can get back to work.

Seems like self respect has become
rare as black diamonds. I'll keep digging, though it seems
hopeless. Something in me won't let me give upon them.

I believe it's that external heartbeat that i feel in my feet. From our first mother... Earth.

Maybe

I just wanted to bleed her.
I wanted my heart to pump her throughout my body,
transferring her to each part of my vessel.

When I prick my finger, she will
understand me better. It will be impossible. Maybe, just
maybe, she will learn to love again.

Bad Bitch from Queen

I know she wonders when the change from Queen to Bad
Bitch took place. In her heart, it never changed and mine
either. What happen to the Kings?

Thoughts that run cross mind, as she is disrespected several
times just walking down the street.

You hear a "beep beep" & quick whistle, with lips that part to
say "nice ass" and blown kisses that are so filled with ill intent
your stomach twists in disgust.

So much for the "What Would Jesus Do" bumper sticker. I'm
sure he wouldn't do that, if he existed.

Who knew her curves would be her curse and her cursing her
curves because of what media portrayed as unhealthy.
Fighting an uphill battle she still overcomes.

All she ever wanted was to be kissed under the moonlight, told
she was beautiful for more than her figure while watching

shooting stars go by. There's a lot behind those brown eyes; intelligence is one of them, pain is the next.

It pains a Queen to look around and see that her fellow women have lost themselves. One day they will wake up, change perspectives and fight, demand respect, equal rights and unite.

Until then her guard is up awaiting better days.

Nikki

My body moves to the rhythm
That is not heard by all.
Toes tap to my heart's song
While my soul is preparing for it's
Moment in the spotlight.

My palms to the ground,
Feeling for the beat of the earth
So my thighs can mimic the vibration.
The heat intensifies
As my body is preparing
For this poetic motion.

I am a dancer,
You can call me Freedom.

I am the epitome of free
When I fly through the sky
Or when I tumble on the earth
Doing what God instilled in me.

To dance is not just an action.
It's a way of life for me.
It is my breath,
My center,

My peace.

I am home in the rhythm, so I invite you home with me. Just
as long as you don't break my groove.
I am in tune on this dance floor.
I am sultry, sexual.
Beautiful & exceptional.

In my dance, I am me.
And with dance, I am free.
No restrictions.

Waiting To Be Mended

There's still love in me,
But it's surrounded by betrayal.
The constant let down of humanity has me feeling like an
angel that fell Too in love with a human
Only to get my wings clipped, in turn.

I would've still accepted the human, but after what was desired
Was taken, you left too.

I know that I am beautiful.
I know that I am a Queen.
I'm also humble and only wish for the simple things.

Why is this not taken in consideration, in matters of the heart?
Actions are made that make me fear love.

I'm so doubtful, but still so hopeful.
I contradict it all.
I am torn,
Waiting to be mended.

Detrimental

If I made love to you
Like I wanted you
To stay,
Would you stay?

Or would you love
The love in the moment
And not care about what
I'm trying to offer you forever?

Either way, you'd be
Detrimental to my being.
It's up to you how
The moment will be
Remembered.

Utter heartbreak,
Or timeless happiness.

Stay (Bed sheets)

Me and you stuck in sheets.
Fucking like rabbits
And we barely want to eat.

Love is our food source.
Baby I need you.
Baby I need we.

Stay in these bed sheets,
This could be our home base.

Lovin all day,
Kisses on your forehead.
You really should stay.

Kisses on your stomach,
Do you really have to go?

Kisses on your thigh,
That's your favorite spot, I know.

She moans "no", so means "yes".
Or did she moan "no"
And mean "sex"?

Either way,
I missing you.
You haven't even gone, yet.

I'm sad now.
Yup. I'm sad now.

Puzzle Pieces

It was the light
That made
Me grateful,
Because it let
Me see her deeply.

Her aura
Matched mine;
It completed me.
Puzzle Pieces.

Stroke Her Soul

Sometimes you need to wake up and praise your woman like the queen she is.

Take her, tell her she's beautiful and taste her again. Caress her body like it is the softest, most out of this world texture you've ever felt.

Tell her you love her flaws until they become her qualities. Love her. Kiss her like you have to leave and you want to remember the moment, then taste her again.

Rub her sides, rub her calves, rub her feet. While you rub her feet, kiss the top of them so she'll feel like royalty. Let that morning be about her.

People say it's good to stroke the ego sometimes, but I'd rather skip that and stroke her soul. Leave that lasting impression of love.

Good morning.

Just Want To Love you

I just want to love you.
I want to pour the contents of my heart out on a table so you see it only contained one thing. You.

You alone were enough to sustain me. You made blood pump through veins that gave life. No pain. Instead, beautiful meaning.

You made me feel again. For the first time my senses were active. To see you was the defining point that verified God was real. If you were made in her image, heaven must be amazing.

It makes no difference though, I have you. To hear you is humbling, with all your vast knowledge you still take your time with me.

To smell you was like being surrounded by every single beautiful flower and the wind taking it's time to blow each scent at you separately so you can have a chance to appreciate them all.

To touch you is to be a part of you, and to be a part of you is to be a part of the world. When I held your hand, it was like being able to visit each of the 7 wonders in one place. Looking into your eyes, seeing the universe, solidified my feelings on you being the 8th.

There's just something about you that secures me and makes me want more of you.

To taste, well...

That Person

I just wanted to be that person
You thought about
When the rain comes down.

The one you wished had their
Arms around you,
As you pretended to be
Able to count raindrops

To clear your mind
From the loneliness and more
On when we embrace again.

Hold Me Down

All I ask is that you hold me down.

Baby I don't want much, just you.
Be my peace, cuz I need you.

Never leave me lonely, just nourish me. I promise to do the
same.

You got me, I got you...

This Bowl

What's mine is yours.
All I want, in return, is your existence.

Love me like you know I have a short time to breathe.
Forgive me when I fall short of your grace.
I'll love you like my body needs you.
You're my nourishment to feed.

My smile consists of you.
When I speak, your spirit will be in my words to insure I won't
disrespect you.
Your time is timeless; shit TIME magazine refused to do an
article on you because they didn't know how to categorize
you!

"Greatness!" I replied, "and no other".

Your beauty was undiscovered - until now. It's mine. All mine.

I don't mean to be possessive, I just appreciate you. Never have I seen a woman who made her blemishes beautiful. I truly feel there's nothing you can't do.

So, share this bowl with me as a symbol of life. Let us make magnificent creations together. Stir and I'll join you.

Take Me To Zion

I just want to feel that empty space...

Take me to Zion.

Let me meet the peace that
Resides in you.

Give me life.
Let me hear the echoes
Of your heart
Then fill that space
With certainty.

Take me to Zion...

On Paper

After everything
Was said and done,
She stayed by my side
Just like poetry did.

For that,
She will live forever
In my heart
Like words written on paper.

Beautiful Death

Her love was the most
beautiful death.

If only to be reincarnated
back into her embrace
to die once more;

I'd do it in a heartbeat...

February 6th

10 years ago,
I met my wife
On Super Bowl Sunday.

It was February 6th.
I had seen her before,
But this was
The first time we spoke in person
And

67

The last time we were ever apart.

It, literally, felt like
I had entered a relationship
That we both refused
To acknowledge,
But both knew we were in.

Seven months later,
She became my wife.

All this time has passed
And
She's still my everything.

- behind every Poet, there is a story...

Abundance

Who really wants to go through
life feeling empty?

Who wants the loneliness of
solitude, when the other half of
your soul is in the world waiting
on you?

Who can smile and lie at the same
time, half way complete, knowing
something is missing?

Not me, I need my love in abundance.

I'm Lonely Without You

My lotus, I grow weak in your absence. Beauty has no real meaning when you have left from eyesight. Food has lost its feeling of nourishment. The sun set that we used to enjoy, has brought, me only sadness. The sunrise we made love under made me feel even more alone.

I grip tightly to the blanket you used to wrap up in to sit and listen to my poetry. I inhale, trying to take in any feeling of you being close to me. I am finding it harder and harder to appreciate life when you are what gives me life.

That is the true reason behind why I call you my lotus. I hope in time I receive a reply, because these days you are away are literally killing me.

Anata ga inaito sabishii desu... (I'm lonely without you...)

Lost key

Smeared makeup, waterfalls start as streams but, this time, they were created from heartbreak.

Soul in disarray, he told me he lost my key and did not want to find it again, lied to me again, said he would protect the key to my heart with his life; guess he died again.

Facts conflict with denial, creating confusion because I'm in disbelief of my reality. This has to be an alternate dimension where all sad things happen to me and soul mates break promises. Like the pilgrims who broke break with Amerindians in the name of peace; but no peace ensued, just

69

pieces of me scattered and diseased with the sickness of sadness.

I am torn... I am torn and my eyes won't stop creating waterfalls. I'm drowning in sorrow and you're standing there with a face and look dry as desserts. Like our love meant nothing. I thought my kisses were irreplaceable. I thought my hugs gave you hope.

Who's going to play in my hair? Who's going to kiss me before bed, like you do? Never thought I had to imagine counting the stars with anyone else but you.

Now all I have are moments I can grab temporary happiness from, that now end in pain. The thought of you hurts, but oddly keeps me sane.

"What makes you laugh can make you cry" has never been more real, than in this moment.

I'm hurting; my mind is in a thick fog so I do what I do best, I skate. I skate to escape it all. I skate to feel free and unbroken. I am free. Picture from model and complete bad ass.

My Day

I know this is my day to rejoice
for love & companionship,
but I want every person to
know love like this.

To know they have a piece
of life's beautiful desire.
Someone to love you back.

Pure

How can I be taken seriously
about respecting a woman's spirit
if I can't even respect the vessel
 that holds it?

If I am to be followed, I shall make sure my actions are pure.
After all, how can I not love the very thing that birthed
creation?

Soul sistah, I love you.

Alone

I wanted to just exist and be left
alone.
When I got what I wanted,
it wasn't what I wanted at all.

Now I sit wishing I had someone to
sit with. Someone to call my own.
.

Learn to Love

I just wanted to bleed her.
I wanted my heart to pump her throughout my body,
transferring her to each part my vessel.

When I prick my finger, she will
understand me better. It will be impossible. Maybe, just
maybe, she will learn to love again.

Vibrations

I prayed before I ate you, I gave your Yoni the glory and
thanked you for you. Your energy wowed me. It was like
drinking directly from the Nile Valley river and finally feeling
a sense of fulfillment. You replenish me with every moan,
every time you told me don't stop, you gave me more life. It
was hard to keep away from you, sweetest chocolate ever
tasted as I soaked in your melanin bath of ecstasy. Your
vibration kept me high, if I didn't know any better I'd had
sworn we went to another dimension with that last ascension
or should I say climax we both felt internally different. It was
peace, a moment of silence was caught while legs were
wrapped around head and you just sat in bliss. These were the
moments that were cherished and remembered while feasting
on you in the morning

What If

Something about you being forbidden calls to me. It breaks
through my resistance and sends me to ecstasy. Lust was never
a factor in our equation; it was always more behind our lying
eye that refused to be honest with our hearts. Being inside of
you was more than penetration. It was a connection that was
built stronger with each stroke and kiss we shared. So what if
we love? What if we forever...

Free

I am free if I choose to be free.
I control how heavy the weight
Feels that I have to carry
I say what goes and what stays
In order of importance
I can feel light as a feather
Or heavy an a ton
I choose the feather ever time
I am in control so I am free

Truly

The only thing that ever
TRULY
felt tangible was the
LOVE
I felt in your embrace.
YOU
keep my heart beating.

Who

Who do I complain to when I myself am the issue...

Remember you

When we first met I made love to you. Not in the literal sense, it was in my heart. Images in my mind played on my heart like a projection screen, it felt so natural to kiss you so passionately with legs intertwined arms locked around neck with nothing between us but drips of moisture that gave off the sweetest of smells. How can this moment be pictured so vividly with me just meeting you but, feeling like I've met you before? Why is my heart protruding through my chest like the first time my first crush spoke to me? How can my heart see you as being familiar with no eyes and I gaze upon you in plain sight and still be unaware of our connection. Maybe if I held you like I did in my heart the secrets of this mystery would be revealed. I wish I had the courage to tell you I've loved you from a past life but I don't. The level of rejection would be too great, I turn to walk away while my heart is heartbroken at the steps I take away from destiny. As the long walk begins an angel taps me on my shoulder and says "I think I know you" I reply "I think I might know you too".

Shooting Stars

She wanted my melanin. She begged for me to transfer my masculine energy insider her and show her how stars were created in the universe. She yearned to be bathed in my moonlight. Her yoni shined for me like galaxies and I took her in like lungs do air. I could hear her pineal gland decalcify as our love continued to transcend past what was expected, into what was needed. Our combined energy turned into love flames under the moonlight. It was no stopping what was already predestined, so let me please you to no end and let us forever remember this moment of love. Moonlighting in melanin.

Daily Love

Daily because I love you. Not only do I love you; I believe in you. I don't love your appearance, I love your soul. I see beyond the shell, beyond the restrictions of normal sight. I want your happiness and I'll do what's needed to get it.

Find my way

I unknowingly lost sight of your worth.
In doing so I lost sight of my own.
This is where I felt less of myself
& more of the person I never imagined
 I'd become.

When I Hurt You

Restlessness is not a term that most would consider to equate with sadness. However, in this restless moment what eases my mind is being in the comfort of your presence. Holding you always gave me spiritual peace, I could feel your soul's embrace. Now that I've hurt you, what I feel is a deep void; a pain that reflects my love as if it's not worthy of you, not good enough to feel your undying devotion or the warmth that comes with it. I am stuck in a prison of my own doing, weather I have reason or not means little now.
All I want is to touch your hand through this glass,
Instead I'm tormented by my own thoughts of what could have been if I would have been better. My heart hurts, my soul is weak, there is no balance, when there is no you. I have to do better for myself so my light can be seen again. I am ready to love you like you always knew I could; just please take the steps with me....

Layers

breath of love. heart filled
With unanswered passion.
Love is under her layers
Of pain, beauty is in
Her soul

Leave Me

I chose death over life in an instant because her existence
wasn't a part of the deal.
What was taking breaths without her love attached to every
inhale, what is the meaning of life without her presence. there
is none so leave me deceased..

Untitled

One of the hardest things I ever had to experience was
receiving the pain from each woman I scarred as I admitted
the hurt I caused....

Winter

I enjoy the warmth needed from another. It's an excuse to be
close. No one shows you how to love like winter.

Favorite

You are my favorite everything. You make me feel materialistic by how much I'm infatuated with you and I don't care. Your soul has set me on fire and I never want to be put out.

Outshine

There were few things in the world that overshadowed a sunset. You were one of them.
Never knew how you did it, but you made the sun seem so miniscule compared to you.

Raise your Consciousness

A lot of men claim to want a conscious woman but not every man is willing to raise their vibration to keep her.

ACKNOWLEDGMENTS

This book has taken me years to create.
It honestly started as an idea that I quickly put away due to fear of failure before I even tried.
I had given up on writing until I met my wife. She gave me the motivation to pick a pen up again. Without her, there would be no PoetOfWar. I love you Goddess.
First I'd like to thank the creator, because without her nothing is possible.
Thank you Maritza for assisting in the long hours of editing and constant rewrites. Going over my poems with a fine tooth comb and being an all around dedicated person to the success of my book.
Dr. Mika thank you for showing me word flow, passion, consistency and how to add the ancestors to everything I do.
Kerrica thank you for always motivating me, searching for venues to do poetry and teaching me about gorilla marketing. Always making me Boss Up!
Travis and Devon thank you for believing in my poetry and getting my project off the ground.
Thank you to those who helped me with my writing, listened to my work & gave me honest feedback.
April Dawone Clecquot Michael Maya menber Dom Melissa Jeannea Nadine Jade Juniper Trina Jamie Rayne Leana Delma Joy Yashna Dani Rebecca Gidgette Zaire Tashanya Boo & Salaama.
Last but not least two of my teacher's that were detrimental to my writing Mr. Mika Lewis and my Poetry teacher Mrs. Lauren Blouin
Words had no real meaning until I was shown how to use them like a paintbrush on a canvas. You both never judged me; showed me love and how to turn my emotions into art. I will always be in your debt.

www.ingramcontent.com/pod-product-compliance
Lightning Source LLC
LaVergne TN
LVHW051605080426
835510LV00020B/3144